RITUAL, INTERRUPTED

RITUAL, INTERRUPTED

POEMS

David Ly

Palimpsest Press
1171 Eastlawn Ave.
Windsor, Ontario. N8S 3J1
www.palimpsestpress.ca

Printed and bound in Canada
Cover design and book typography by Ellie Hastings
Edited by Jim Johnstone
Cover Illustration by Jess Stanley

Palimpsest Press would like to thank the Canada Council for the Arts and the Ontario Arts Council for their support of our publishing program. We also acknowledge the assistance of the Government of Ontario through the Ontario Book Publishing Tax Credit.

Anstruther Books

Canada Council for the Arts | Conseil des Arts du Canada
ONTARIO ARTS COUNCIL | CONSEIL DES ARTS DE L'ONTARIO
an Ontario government agency | un organisme du gouvernement de l'Ontario
CERTIFIED CANADIAN PUBLISHER
Canada
ONTARIO CREATES | ONTARIO CRÉATIF

LIBRARY AND ARCHIVES CANADA CATALOGUING IN PUBLICATION

TITLE: Ritual, interrupted : poems / David Ly.
NAMES: Ly, David, author.
IDENTIFIERS: Canadiana (print) 20260235768
Canadiana (ebook) 20260235776
ISBN 9781997508199 (SOFTCOVER) | ISBN 9781997508205 (EPUB)
SUBJECTS: LCGFT: Poetry.

CLASSIFICATION: LCC PS8623.Y22 R58 2026 | DDC C811/.6—DC23

For everyone learning to live with interruption.

TABLE OF CONTENTS

SUMMON

SEVER

RESURRECT

SUMMON

INCANT

You've texted enough to know you can't have
any kind of meaningful conversation with
yourself.

Messaged into the aether
like you're saying goodbye to voices only you
can hear.

You sense them, don't
you? A kiss on the back of your neck, bite
marks on your shoulder

to keep you from keeling
over, even though you're already on the bathtub
floor.

This phone isn't a
planchette. And these words aren't magic – at
best

they're doorways, black
portals where the summoned will

stay.

CONJUREBEAST

Four seconds on the inhale, then six
to breathe out while holding yourself
together. You've never been this
ravenous to break loose. No will left
to hold it back any longer, vapor slips

out between your teeth, ribbons
around your neck, turns sharp at your
throat as you greet the beast that
reminds you feathers aren't just
tender, but can cut before they caress.

PAIN / DOOR

Nobody else. No one else can cut into you. The hurt only bearable when you hurt yourself, ritualistic distraction from frustration that cannot be lessened otherwise. Those first droplets are the most potent: the perfect offer pooling in dirty grout. Say it in your mind: away. A way. Out. Make it. Make a way. Out. Say it until blood glows black along the edges of the tile. Now press. Press your fists to the floor. Push through the door. No one else can push through your hurt.

A SCAVENGER

~~exists~~ ~~is born~~ ~~calls out~~ circles above on fleshy wings searching for company, clutching ~~something~~ ~~someone~~ you within its talons for safekeeping, ~~holder~~ ~~guardian~~ ~~saviour~~ keeper of all that is ~~you~~ hidden, especially what you don't want to ~~hold~~ see, happily ~~taking~~ consuming, surgically ~~stealing~~ scavenging until you feel grounded though at least some ~~intricacies~~ parts of yourself that you hate still ~~exist~~ breathe – whenever you ~~know~~ feel like any part of you should not exist, it is ~~correct~~ safe to ~~love~~ succumb to the shadow that looms, that has forever followed, winged, always silent, waiting, ~~hungrily~~ empathetically circling above, talons ready to tear you from your ~~nightmare~~ thoughts.

INFINITY IN MIND

My mind void of self-compassion, I make a den for the serpent seeking refuge to safely coil around

itself and not be prey to ~~hypotheses~~ judgment. I know how helpful it is to feel ~~accepted~~ safe in

order to explore why I hurt, unable to name my pain unless provided the necessary protection against it,

the ~~voice~~ serpent comes to choke my thoughts, a reminder that ~~it~~ I need a moment not to lunge

at opportunities for escape, but instead remain here in my discomfort as the serpent can be skittish. No

sudden ~~movements~~ dilemmas while it swallows its tail. It ~~wants~~ needs to eat, so let it eat.

NO STRAYING

I let my demons run free in dreams / *through all pathways* / They return with me to the waking world / *through all pathways, no destination* / Walk with me / *don't trail behind* / I am all pathways / *we do not need a destination*

THE DEVIL

I often think about the devil:
how he's one card drawn
for my past, the one card
that haunts my future.

After each reading, I stop—

keeping him away would be
useless if I saw more:
if he were waiting for me down
the road, or if he's been

by my side this entire time.

SELF-PERCEPTION AS SYLLOGISMS

I

Moments of frustration are bats learning to echolocate.
My bedridden evenings are moments of frustration.

∴ My bedridden evenings are bats learning to echolocate.

II

Self-pollinating bee orchids are self-actualized.
Some desires are like self-pollinating bee orchids.

∴ Some desires are self-actualized.

III

Dragons have a way of making me feel real.
Not all future imaginings have a way of making me feel real.

∴ My future imaginings are not all dragons.

IV

My feelings of unexplained agitation are flightless birds.
Some flightless birds are not fantasies.

∴ Some fantasies are not feelings of unexplained agitation.

V

My intrusive thoughts don't have raptor claws.
The worlds I escape to for safety are intrusive thoughts.

∴ The worlds I escape to for safety don't have raptor claws.

FEELS LIKE IMAGES

cutting their way out of my skull with serrated incisors, falling out as these words – I know there are others that haunt me with sharper teeth – how do they read? A pallid bat echolocates, finds the stinger of Scorpius – an image that I haven't fully seen yet is hidden within its cave, remains until I am confident enough to reach in – I may never be – more images arrive at the foot of my bed – I wish I could recall their initial forms – now there are obsidian antlers, faceless faces – asking how I could conjure them to only exist in my mind – they make me feel a bit less lonely – imbuing my selfhood with teeth and sharp silhouettes standing between me and the self I refuse to see.

BRING ME THE BEAST, LIVE

The mayhem once missed, I now
hungrily enter its funeral mouth,
the flood of venomous green
light that urges me to sing back
to the screen, to the black horns
bowing before your face

is unveiled

becoming a skull awash in gold
among opera house ruins, my
shadow swaying and screaming
for the beast, the animal, the
monster, the life, live—

THE FIRST SPELL

was conjured when humans looked at the moon.

We pointed up so that more of us would see
(and we haven't stopped talking about it since).

CHAOS

He didn't believe
in his magic's
potency

until his rat trap
caught a tiny
sparrow.

That's why
you shouldn't
set spells

and forget
about their
power

he repeated
until he could
see feathers

closing
the eyes of
his mind

WISHING INTO THE BLUE

I find it difficult to avoid
the darkness

like a fish rippled
with the sky's reflection

evading the dagger-like

                    beak of a blue heron.

I spoke so surely to you

when I said:

see a heron, make a wish

because it's what I needed:

a made-up spell
to heal

cast upon feathers

the eye of the storm
that's set its sights on me.

If only I put as much effort
into bettering myself as I do
in imagining
impossible ways to do so.

If only I wasn't

the fish, veil-finned and skittish, plagued with panic when my skies grey.

Maybe

it's time to [re]make myself in the form of the heron.

Before the storm, I could
patiently stand under the sky

over the water

until a disturbance
washes
through the sky's reflection

quietly strikes it

with the precision of lightning,

electric blue
shooting up
into the storm.

WHAT WORLDS DO U DREAM OF?

I'm so inexplicably irritated these days, unnerved as if I'm always running to catch a bus, the one that looks as if it's a wall

with dripping pink letters that read "What worlds do u dream of?" As a child, I imagined myself existing elsewhere,

anywhere there were voices other than the ones that reprimanded me for being too quiet. I think I didn't begin talking until age

three. The two of us feel similar: trying to remain unseen, not even imagining ourselves in others, and now I escape in the

books you gifted, the ones where dragons *slip between* dimensions. This year, I read about Duluth, first to *slip between* with his

rider, never to be seen again. A quiet heartbreak, the gift of other worlds, a self sometimes caught between them.

THE LEGACY

is carried on carrion wings / a shimmer of bioluminescence between orange leaves / in found-again summoning circles. The legacy begins when the last offering goes willingly / defiantly / blissfully / in a promise / from a broken covenant. The legacy is a stranger's palm soothing the fright / untrustworthy comfort. The legacy grows when something stands in a dark corner playing pretend in a human-like silhouette / in a form unable to be imagined again. The legacy is a ghost / beast / dream made flesh / acknowledgment that we breathe.

SEVER

COVEN CALLS

My coven calls, reaches through the years to say that I have strayed too far from ~~home~~ myself, hexed with guilt that weighs me to the mattress. Wellness is capricious magic. I have yet to untangle myself from the knotted blanket of its incantations.

SILVER AND BLUE

Do you still think about the nightmare where you drowned? The one where you're the dream, where you're drenched upon waking, waiting to be taken under again? You always did prefer the familiar.

Frozen at four in the morning, its too early for the day to begin, and far lonelier into any night you want be awake in.

DROMAEOSAURIDAE

Feathers and sickle claws. As in my claws are sharp: kept retracted, they multiply when needed. I hunt in disemboweling silences where down-like feathers litter the living room carpet. As in I did not cut. Chose cutting words. As in I failed to cut myself away. A way free. As in I was too quiet. Not bloodthirsty enough for the safety of the koi pond. As in why must our claws be sharpened on one another? As in within this family of raptors. Am I the only one who marvels at our feathers? I desired to grow more into the sky, unknowingly promised myself flight. As in I am beyond gliding, I am beyond the sickle claws at my throat.

LONELY HEXES

Spells are ephemeral:
the closer you come
the further I want to be
from myself

CARCASS

Touch started as a murmur
soft   child-like   then bellowing
with aggression   unignorable
until I wrote to it   scratching
                                        your   name
                              into this paper spine
                              all skittish   antlered
but in need.
Now I'm inside, elbow-deep
                    trying to pull the beating out
                    reaching for something other
                         somewhere beyond time
fingertips slipping through
the warm viscous embrace
of splintered ribs
                              in a carcass riddled
                                        with holes
until finally   it is quiet
no murmurs no bellowing no meaning.

FFS, HOW SCARY IS THAT?

You still think about yourself as a chain of terrifying events that cannot be clarified. Tornado, tsunami, tempus fugit. You are fearful to peer back, but more so you simply cannot – your fear, the terror of wakefulness lighting the way to a dreamless world.

CHANNELING

The only thing SAD lighting does is make you fantasize about being underground, held beneath then released, pressure upon your chest to rival what pushes from behind your ribs, the sensation that says breath is unfit for life. I know, it doesn't mean you want the grave early, rather, just to be lowered into the dirt, away from all sound, whispering in someone else's voice with more conviction and familiarity than your own.

ECHOLESS

I wake in early-evening guilt, a ghost bat beholden to another broken covenant / Rest always cures me but the cost is waking in an unfamiliar form, discovering that my nose-leaf fails to focus my echolocation / Even if I could fly I wouldn't be able to discern the exact whereabouts of food, water, still straining in human ways to behave / Manners should be natural according to my new body's capabilities / Beyond quiet chirps that loudly ring in my pointed ears as calls of distress seemingly inaudible to others.

NARRATIVE ATTEMPT

It's not what or who you are, but it has your silhouette all spiky and sharp with long, mantis-like limbs. Keep it contained to one spot in the room. Tell it, *please stay on the ceiling, in the corner with the philodendron.* It might not do what you ask, but let it remain external, up there until it finishes sulking, until you let your guard down, forgetting that it watches hundreds of you through compound eyes. It's not what or who you are – dagger arms at the ready to pierce the neck – but it's who you're fearful of becoming.

BURNOUT / HIGH UNDER HEAVEN

Wildfire smoke does not simulate
the sensation of flying through

clouds like I imagined it would. Red
eyes. A red giant. I begin the

process of dying each evening:
expect to feel more in my body

with a deep breath. Instead, is this
how it feels to leave myself? I

inhale a bit too intensely, smoke-
choked, and open my eyes to see

my body from above: a constellation
until fully burnt away.

ETERNAL HUNTERS

Then

Death would cast its circle around me that day, leaving little time to decide if the end should enter by way of Wolf's teeth or upon Lamb's swift, unwavering light-tipped arrows: both sensed me coming apart as I quivered, their next mark. Bow raised with anticipation for surrender, there's nothing to be done but sigh with relief as Lamb danced her feather-heavy arrows into my chest.

Now

I pull arrows out of my chest, crush them between the ground and my palm. Silver rings around me: Lamb laughs as I reverse Death's cycle and Wolf circles, livid that he may not feel me within his mouth. Not here, not yet. I remain on the blood-blessed ground waiting for the veil to fade. I step through, dance between arrows, turn the hunt back onto them, Lamb huffing, "Now, Wolf."

LIMINAL

Everything feels the same – there's no miracle that will pull the panic from behind your ribs, no sacrifice great enough to leave upon the altar, so you return to box breathing.

Decay is in the air. Panic destroys relief, urges every breath to be shallower than the last. The last seals when it should open, the last binds you within a box of your own making – the last sacrifice stirs its wings upon the altar.

SUFFOCATION SPELL

Exposed, suddenly everything inside of you
is a bit jittery. Impatient. Manageable until

claustrophobia starts to creep in. Out in
the open on this balcony you feel

the suffocation spell, unintentionally set
because you couldn't catch your breath.

Whenever life feels cosmic, like it can easily
crush your existence, you're never at fault

for coveting your safety, forging protection
as stubborn as the wards in the sky. But now

look up: they've begun to fade and it's okay to
smile – their purpose stirs within their conjurer.

HOW TO

apologize? The words seem as insincere as winged carrion eaters that won't land on rotting flesh. Which muscle does it take to avoid feeling selfish for speaking with self-compassion? To make sense of myself? I've tried, sinews deteriorating, and in the gloaming, the glow of star-bleached bones, a void where my heart once grew.

RESURRECT

NECROMANTIC

Necromancy is performed under moonlight
Necromancy in the birds, feathered shadows of theropods
The face of an orchid each year: necromancy
Like an angel – except necromancy pierces me with talons
Through necromancy, unexpected futures are divined
I feel another's necromantic presence within me
Bloody vulture heads smell of necromancy
I consider necromancy a living suit, way to persevere
Necromancy: walking and breathing with every thought
Necromancy is sunshine sealed inside of me

FLORENCE

I'm picking up where we left off last night: each lyric a grimoire, each lyric a dark November morning. Your layered howls soothe the scraping in my skull. Did I forget to take my headache pill? On this particular morning I'm not falling as hard, but still wonder how my world will collapse if I come to the end of loving myself. I can't quite imagine inhabiting it now, with this spell around me. I'm safe and tethered here for a rest, no more drifting on the pacific wind: each lyric a grimoire, each lyric a dark November morning.

VIOLET

You may not feel good about meeting again, but you can't deny it's comforting and familiar: moist ground cradling your body after the fall, consumed by glowing purple vines as I swoop through mist, lilac wings stirring the air trying to claim you –

Which secret ritual did you fail to perform? Did you starve the persistent cravings that disturbed your loves? Ignore your emptiness? I want you to live – let me re-awaken the violet in your veins each time we kiss, the tenacity you need to grow your own wings.

TENSE

Do you feel loved? I'm time travelling, casting fear into the future – I hold it with my worries, carry its tension in my shoulders, even with your small arms around me. You may not exist but time will not stop, does not worry how we feel, only that we must feel all of the way through to live, and for me to make way for you to live too.

CHIROPTEROPHILY

A night-blooming flower is ~~pollinated~~ kissed by a nectar bat. What must this feel like. A cave. A secret vow. It's wings ~~soar~~ still while a new moon looms into view. The ~~darkness~~ heartbeat is sapped from the sky. Long tongues dive into petals. An entire night is ~~taken~~ sweet, pollen-dusted ~~bodies~~ anthers proliferate.

SOME DAYS

an exhale makes disappearing feel plausible, and you forget that you're still breathing as if breath doesn't make space for living / Some days you cry because this is what cowardice must feel like, holding perfectly still, the impossibility of choice in the bathtub as water burns your back / Some days you tell me that it isn't enough, this life, and no, it isn't, but some days the possible is a little less impossible.

ENOUGH TO CUT

You break the seal that we were warned never to touch. Glass slips from your hands and we stand while crows drop around us. You ask if there will be any ground left as songs that made it easier to breathe fade from memory. Whatever notes they leave behind are more resolved than they should be. We have never been confident in the sureness and safety of silence. But understand, you didn't break the seal by accident. You didn't wade into the quiet afterward because you were afraid of what might answer back. You hoped glass would be sharp enough to cut your fear away.

CONSIDER THIS PROOF OF LIFE

After ~~death~~ I survive myself

WORLD EATER

Peer up at lights of long-gone celestial bodies until Jupiter floats into view: a dense core cradling traces of younger worlds consumed during its growth: planet cannibalization concealed by a Van Gogh-like atmosphere. Through a lens a great red storm gazes back at you: a conglomeration of all the spaces you've inhabited: spaces that touched you while you hurtled through the cosmos. Space contains nebulae where you breathed when a breath was most needed, a surging force all on your own. Never look into the eyes of old gods unless ready to taste your next world.

WHOLE PICTURE

__________ must be cunning
__________ was ~~sneaky~~ afraid

no need for ~~spells~~ __________
intend for the ~~best~~ __________
end up with ~~joy~~ __________

ORNITHOPHILY

A ~~weight~~ seed in the chest and its ~~gravity~~ ~~presence~~ song is noticed like the black of a ruby-throated hummingbird ~~teasing~~ ~~flashing~~ exploding with iridescent red when glimpsed from a new angle. The desire to see it again grows when I walk a bit lighter, falling out of myself like pollen blown from the center of a ~~poppy~~ lily.

CARRION

Tear away with precision,
don't damage
what's
left
or assume
that what remains
is no good.

Latch on to a morsel if impulse
can't be controlled –
only what is
wanted
imbues worth,
parts of a salvageable self
filled with
once-thought rot.

THE NIGHTMARE, REVERSED

He tries to commune with me by pouring salt over a bat skull, a flutter of panic in his chest each time I flick the candlelight blue. Imagine moving through life with a force that sews bespoke suffering? A personal deity of chaos. A long-overdue talk. He has only one question, unable to decide between desiring me destroyed, bound, or set aflame if I materialize, forgetting that he imagines me invisible so I am nowhere to be sensed. He stands, crushes the bat skull, perceives my absence, and leaves me uncrowned.

RITUAL, INTERRUPTED

I watch from below through the sheen of warm blood flowing out of a reptilian bird: my focus and jawline so sharp that I feel the sky is cut open and all of my desires are hemorrhaging down. The only sensation throbbing through me is nostalgia for boyish beliefs and hope that a peace-full & still mind remains, but what seeks me out is covered with slate feathers probing my fears. This existence is worth more than everything I desire, and it is only now that I notice my mind has wandered – look: here is the promise to take a breath again, here is the sky releasing the cravings that haunt me, here are my hands, opening.

NOTES

A previous version of "Chaos" won *Arc Poetry Magazine*'s November 2022 Arc Award of Awesomeness.

"Eternal Hunters" is inspired by the character Kindred from Riot Games' *League of Legends.*

ACKNOWLEDGMENTS

Thank you to the following publications for including previous iterations of the following poems in this book:

The Cortland Review, issue 94: "Florence"

carte blanche, issue 49: "Eternal Hunters" (published as "Ode to Kindred, the Eternal Hunters)

Contemporary Verse 2, Summer 2024, vol. 41, issue 1: "World Eater"

SAD Mag Online: "Ritual, Interrupted"

Augur Magazine, issue 6.2: "Dromaeosauridae"

The Fiddlehead, Autumn 2023, no. 296: "Ornithophily" and "Chiropterophily"

Arc Poetry Magazine, November 2022: "Chaos"

THANK YOU

To Jim, Aimée, Ellie, and all at Palimpsest Press for being constant champions of my poetry, Canadian books, and my growth as a writer.

To Jess Stanley for illustrating a beautiful cover from my darkest dreams.

To the Canada Council for supporting this book.

To readers of *Mythical Man* and *Dream of Me as Water* for your indelible support of my work.

DAVID LY is the author of *Mythical Man* (Anstruther Books, 2020) and *Dream of Me as Water* (Anstruther Books, 2022), both shortlisted for ReLit Poetry Awards, and the fantasy novel *Not All Dragons* (Poplar Press, 2026). He is co-editor, with Daniel Zomparelli, of *Queer Little Nightmares* (Arsenal Pulp Press, 2022). His work has appeared widely in anthologies and literary journals, and he is the recipient of *The Ex-Puritan*'s Austin Clarke Prize in Literary Excellence. He is Poetry Editor at *This Magazine* and serves on the editorial board of Poplar Press, the speculative fiction imprint of Wolsak & Wynn.